To Holly

MancunianMeanderMikeGarry

MikeGarry x

Cheers Ta
Publications

First published in 2006
by Cheers Ta Publications
Cheers Ta House
10 Merston Drive Manchester M20 5WT

All layout and design by Ant Ball Design

A CIP record for this book is available from the British Library
ISBN 0 9536392 23

To John Murphy 1960-2005

Amanda, Maria, Connor, Portia. Leila
Mam, Seamus, Patricia, Theresa, Christopher and Hugh
Maureen, Anna, Norma and Chris
Ziad, Amiera, Munir, Khalid, Claire, Leanne, Nathan, Jordan, Joshua, Liam
Paddy and Nell

Thanks to John Mcloughlin
Ant Ball of Ant Ball Design
(the best book designer in the world)
Mick, Andy and all the Stars in the Summerhouse

Acknowledgments

Mancunian Meander has been published in Pulp, City Life, The Big Issue, Manchester Evening News, Irish Post, Daily Sport, Lampton Court.

It has been performed in a thousand Venues from the Nuyorican Poets Cafe, Manhattan to Zaal 100 in Amsterdam.

Mancunian Meander has been read on BBC Radio 4, GMR and All FM. And God Created Wythenshawe was a community play devised by Louise Wallwein

All photography by Amanda McCrann and Mike Garry

Contents

Manchester Haiku p1

Mancunian Meander p2

Man Running p6

Regeneration p15

Murphy p18

Flying Bikes over Merseybank p22

Beards p25

Reginald Varney p29

The Fallow Field p35

Don't Rush Home p39

City Living p42

And God Created Wythenshawe p45

Embarrassed to be Half-English p52

Think About It P56

Manchester Haiku

Football fans slumber
Imagining miracles
A curious joy

Tea in the Wine bar
Chips and curry from the chinese
Trams in the bus lane

Wry smiles from grey skies
Streets paved in paving stones
People cast in gold

Mancunian Meander

Gorton girls know all the words
To songs by Chaka Khan
They dance and sing
And point and grin
At all the boys covered in tattoos
Trainers gleaming
Faded denim
Twisting a sleeper in one ear
Driving XR3's and growing home-grown weed
Following the Kippax cheer

But only girls gyrate in Gorton
The boys are making plans
To rid themselves of the CSA
And move to Amsterdam

Jump on the 53
Give the driver 70p
Alight at the DSS
Welcome to Rusholme
What a sorrowful mess
This is Asia town South Manchester
Or is it central now?
Where you can buy the most exotic fruit
And vegetables
Half cows
In the evening the place is heaving
There's a thousand restaurants to fill
Poppodoms, Madras and water
Then quickly shown the bill

But behind this tacky facade
Little Johnny plays in his ten-foot yard
Slapping his Mam's head off the wall
Because there's nowhere to play

In Rusholme anymore
Just a park full of needles
Dog dirt, johnnies and smack dealers
Deprived, ignored and forgotten
Like the fruit in the alleys - rotten

Get me out of this dive

Jump on the 53
Give the driver 55
Pass the job shop
Where the Ethiopians and the Irish
Are forced to live in a shoebox
They thought they'd escaped the war
On the border of Moss Side and Rusholme
Not at all

Fight your way off the 53
At Rec. park on Great Western Street
And walk in mellow laid-back state
Towards the famous Princess Parkway
Watch the commuters
Driving to their networked computers
Pick up the quids
Then drive home to the wife and kids
And curse the price of childcare
In Wilmslow, Hale and Alderley Edge

Across this Russian roulette road
Is the Alexandra Park estate
A place of beauty and a place of hate
A place of culture and history
Forget the museums charting science and industry
With their millions of pounds from the
National Blaggery
This is a place that you want to be
If it's a better person you want to see

Take a talk down Pepperhill Walk
To fifteen-year-old kids earning 2K a week
Running this and that
Here and there
"Take my mountain bike if you dare
Do you really think I want to do this?
The authorities are taking the piss
So now I sell my dreamy concoction
Because a Moss man's provided
With very few options
Just a paint brush and some overalls
And instructions to paint some old church hall
'But I thought you said you liked art'
Said my careers advisor Mr Marx"

Take a walk down the Quinney chicane
Watch real people dodging pitbulls in the rain
And asking God to ease their strife
Whilst working hard to make a life
When everything in the world is working against
Them

Man Running

A man is running in a vortex of a town
Running so fast he can't slow down
Through streets of cars and sheets of rain
Turn a corner and it's the same street again

A man is running from a city
"Oh my lord, isn't it a pity
You can't come in here without slacks and shoes
Go find yourself a rave or a blues
And find yourself a bloody job"
A silent finger responds to the yob

A man is running
Chased by penguins of vengeance
Pounding ankles and stretching tendons
Crossing concrete roundabouts
The Mancunian Way above
Delroy and Patrick in the subway making love
Muggers stoop silently in the shade
Shaking nervously
Cold and afraid
To confront OAP's in the dull light of night
"Give me your money or I'll hit you - alright?"

A man is dodging mountain bikes and sports cars
Full of men and women talking laa de daa
They pop in and pop out and shout
Sell and buy
From nine to five from Mon to Fri
Taking so much and giving nothing back
Just exhaust fumes, dumped ashtrays
And local people the sack

A man is running over fences and sharks
Laughing at the casual remarks

"Do you wanna buy a video?
Fifty quid
I've got the remote
Come on, our kid
Alright then, just give me thirty
But be quick my man cos I'm going cold turkey"
No thank you Mr. Smack
And please put your Mother's video back.

A man is running through packs of dogs
Forced to wander aimlessly
Forced to scavenge
Forced to hate anything or anyone
Official
"Official bloody lifewreckers" shouts mad Mary
From outside the Red Admiral door
Swigging cider, sprawled on the floor

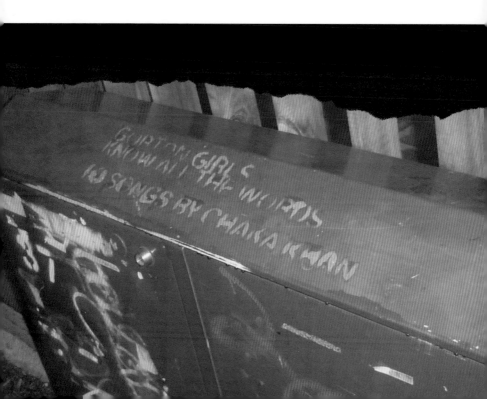

A man is running along the Parkway
The sad smell of hops and the screech of cops
Slows him on his way
Blue lights blinding
Nineteen-year-old words - patronising
"Where are you going, son? Where's the fire?
Have you been drinking?
You fucking liar
Wait till I get you in the back of my van
I'll teach you the difference between a boy
And a man"

A man is running into Medlock Court
Beelzebub would not follow him in there
Full of pinball people, popping and poncing
Dark colonnades, supermarkets of crime
Needles, blood, cum, scum, dirt and grime

"If you're looking for the guy on the 14th floor
He's been busted, he ain't dealing anymore
What do you want?
I've got rock, black or brown
And a knife so sharp
I could cut you down to the ground"

A man is running from a dripping blade
Through Hugh Birley and towards the Nia
Passing homeless people sat around a fire

"Help the homeless, mate, buy my last Issue
Jesus Christ, what has happened to you?
Call an ambulance or hail a taxi
You've got to get yourself to Casualty
Has someone had you with a machete or knife?
Did you get caught stealing yourself a life?"

A man is running to the Factory and the PSV
Where once Curtis moaned Devoto groaned
And if you looked real hard you'd see Morrissey
This was Manchester music at it's own christening
Inspiring young artists stood there listening
A place of vibrancy and atmosphere
Where under-age eyes
Watched in amazement and fear
The catalyst for a culture called the Hacienda
Where Wigan, Bury and Rochdale
Used to go on their benders
Good old Anthony confused pound signs and art
With his Cambridge tongue and Salford heart
To' and his mates were fleeced
Never wanting to cash in
And that explains his irritating grin

A man is running passing Tommy Doherty
Of John Nash Crescent
Where friends give each other nooses as presents
"You do not have the faintest idea
Of the pain, stress and tension that comes

From living round here
All sorts of people thrown in together
Most of them nearing the end of their tether
The highest graduate rate in the country
Learn their skills
Think they're cool
For living in poverty
Till the dosh runs out
Then they slyly phone Mummy
With instructions concerning envelopes
Crammed full of money
Too much pain before my very eyes"
Then Tommy tightens the noose and takes a dive

A man is running through Charles Barry
Where poets poeticise poignantly
Artists articulate with authoritatively
Musicians tune their life strings and join a band
Red Stripe and Rizzla
One in each hand
Where prostitutes, pimps and dealers
Are considered upper class
Drinking pints of pina colada in a straight glass
They are viewed by the ignorant as really posh
With Sky, borders and pockets full of dosh

"Its costs money, you know
Wives kids and cars
I've just got an old 65 Jaguar
It's not fast at the lights
But its great with the chicks
I blow the horn, pull over
Then deliver the 'How's it going darling' pitch"

A man is running into the Spinners
Not advisable if you're just a beginner
In the highly skilled art of scoring drugs

Too many blaggers blagging
Too many thugs
They argue and push you and finally scream
In an effort to make you buy a snide £10 weed
Man stops and stares
At all these people selling their wares
Man turns with blood dripping
And runs to the door
Falls over a pram and gets cursed by two whores

A man is running through tramps and trippers
Some who'd make a saint of the Yorkshire Ripper
Old men and old women bent over in pain
Carrying bags with the red words KWIK SAVE
Printed boldly on the side
A full week's shopping for £5.99
Living in fear of being attacked or mugged
Or thrown out of their home by a Housing thug

A man is running by a young single mother
Pushing a crammed three-wheeled double buggy
Three kids
Farley's rusk and ten packs of Huggies
'I've just nicked these nappies from Moss Side
Shopping centre, I'm gonna flog them today
Then go out on a bender
Do an E and forget my real life for the night
Wake up in the morning and do whatever's right
To feed and clothe my kids
They take priority
Fuck the money I owe to the local authority
For rent, fines and Council Tax
That force so many suicides
Jumping on people's backs
Demanding dosh that people round here
Just haven't got"

A man is running passing heroes with every stride
Too many heroes forced to hide
Too many men running from chasing gangs
Crying and frightened, hot gun in hand
Too many women running from a drunken man
Sold the fridge-freezer for a hundred cans
Too many children running from men with cars
Telling stories, giving sweets and leaving scars
A man is running in a vortex of a town
Can't slow down
Can only stop

Regeneration

The golden sun glistens above the dilapidated ruins
That were once humans' homes
Shadows grow as the fiery planet slowly climbs
Its way to the top of the world
Radiating a spot where Mr Rolls lived

Cries of children's laughter
Echo around the building site
Entrancing the wolf that whistles, bares its bum
But rarely bites

A white cooker stands high and alone
On a drumlin of sand, soil and societal sediment
Once the very fabric of people's lives

Green curtains are half-drawn in the glassless
Windows of a second floor flat
And above the chaos of twisted steel
Jagged slabs
Concrete boulders
A yellow workman's hat

Diggers dig and cranes roar
In an attempt to bring the community to the floor
Brick by brick and stone by stone
Pull old buildings down
Build new homes
This is how regeneration begins
People lose
Contractors win
The chaotic destruction of whole communities
All in line with Government policy
Architecturally brainwashing
Generation after generation

Barbed-wire fences and floating dust
Large cranes and plant covered in rust
Builders and joiners from out of town
Tear houses, shops and boozers down
But orders must be carried out to the letter
To please the bosses and make things better

These people who redesign our lives
Live a million miles away with their wives
And kids who play on vast green lawns
Framed by blooming flower beds
But would swap it all for a Sunday with Dad
They are far away from floating dust
Speeding cars that maim and kill
A different kind of hurt
A different kind of pollutionville

And when they have finished their rebuilding
Ex-homeless people begin to move in
They're impressed for a month or two
Then realise that the plastic glue hardboard and formica
That holds this fragile box together
Is just like the princess who scissored the ribbon
On the outside pristine
On the inside a midden

First they find large black cockroaches
Second, big black rats
These houses are built on top of flats
That were built on top of houses
That were built on a bog
Soon they'll begin to bend and bob
Back and forth and side to side
Cracks appear and whole streets slide

Then a rat-like councillor decides
This crime-ridden area of dilapidation
Is in serious need of regeneration
Let's build things up and make things fine
With a grant from sexy Hestletine"

£500 million already spent
And £44.90 collected in rent
Rebuilding doesn't make problems go away
It just creates a new dumping grounds
For the poor, the black, the Irish and the gay.

Murphy

Brooks Bar isn't far
Jump in any Salmon car
Cheapest cabs in Manchester without a doubt
No locks on the doors
No puke on the floor
And no fat bastard driver trying to throw you out

Tell the driver to take you to the party
In leafy green Chorlton-cum-Hardy
Ask him or her to take the long way round
Sit back and listen to the pirate sounds
Slapping out pure dub and reggae
On this your Mancunian away day
On this your Mancunian away day

Enjoy Withington Road
Special schoolgirls by the bus load
Staying late for a detention
Poverty beyond comprehension
Working women in Victorian settings
Not enough child benefit and too much
Scratchcard betting
And Julie shouts
"Don't take the piss, I'm only doing my job

Playing with an old man's throb
Or being a shrink to
Judges, barristers and dibble who think
The more they slap me
The more I'll love them
You wouldn't believe the sorts of geezers
Who walk through my door
Many say they do it simply cos they're bored
A lot of men just want to be held
Really close
Really tight
All night
Some men just want to fight
Mostly, they say, that they do it for a change"
That's life in the slow lane
Welcome to Whalley Range

Swing a right up the Masculine road
Where affluent Asians walk
Dobermans and Alsatians
Aspiring Irish who eat fish on Fridays
Church club on Saturdays
Drink fifteen pints of porter
Worship their god in a church called
The English Martyrs

Take a left at Manchester Road
Dump the fish, tip the driver
Meander and flow
In and out of Chorltons quaint small shops
Brillo pads, clothes pegs, pans and pots
British butchers, Polish bakers and arty farty
Candlestick makers
Smashed windows in the public houses
Gratified walls with the words
              STONE ROSES
Gangs of lads stood outside pubs

Drinking beer in the cold
The sweet smell of burning Afghanistan Gold
Guys ripping the piss out of each other
A symbol of friendship from one to another

Check the Lamplight, known later as the Limit
And the thugs, crooks and bandits
That happen to go in it
They've got many an interesting story to tell
Of sex, scoring and Socialist Workers from hell

Checkout the Spread, the Royal Oak
The Bowling Green and the Horse and Jockey where
Curly can be seen
Loading his wages into a fruit machine
Or sweating over a nag in the 3.15
But please don't sit down in the Trevor
Or you'll be sat in there for bloody ever
With builders, joiners, sparks and actors
And tanned, Pringle jumpered sub-contractors
Hiding from queues of men
Who have waited all day
For a small brown envelope
A full week's wage
That they'll drink and smoke and bet and waste
Adding one more wrinkle to the poor wife's face
Striated with age but with a certain grace
And Beech Road is full of tourists and toads
And the Lead Station
A dolly dikes' nation

Just off Beech Road is the Irish Club
Where the sub-contractors go
When they've sneaked out of the pub
The car park is bulging red Mercedes and Sierras
Paid for with the money that they fleeced
From their brother
Who arrived in Chorlton with a bag

A name and a promise of "the start"
Laying black Tarmacadam in Carrington Spa
They have consciously remembered
To forget their culture
Of working together
Looking after one another
Never taking any leaves from the Asian books
The rich Irish in Manchester rarely give a fuck

Chorlton-cum-Hardy is a wonderful place
Like a smile on a battered and bruised
Child's face
With its pubs and clubs, chippies and shops
And gangs of lads being caught on the hop
And gangs of girls swapping curling tongues
With cousins, mates, aunties and mums

Flying Bikes Over Merseybank

This place is warm
This place is dark
This area of land is like an enormous park
Without the swings, the slides, somersaults and
Mars Bars
Canoodling teenagers and dumped XR3 cars
The crown green bowlers are laid out underground
Under the green their bones can be found
A pointed building is strategically placed
At the top of the drive
Beyond large green gates
Smoke spews out of the chimney all day
Part and parcel of a priesthood
And how to earn a wage

Big black Bentleys
Transport what appear to be gentry
Stood in twos they form a queue
Like dominoes to a pew
And listen to kind words
From a man who speaks kindly of everyone
But knows no-one

Then they'll march really slow
To a hole in the ground
And quietly lower their loved ones quietly down

Meanwhile
Charlie's safe in the car park
Mountain bike hidden in the bushes
Where it's safe and dark
He is carrying an enormous Head holdall
The kind of thing men use for football
He is picking locks and smashing windows
Nicking handbags, jackets and Blaupunct stereos
Ray Ban sunglasses and C.D. players
Old cassettes of Leo Sayer
He'll leave when he has finally filled his bag
With articles known to others as swag
But to thirteen-year-old Charlie
This is his bread and butter
He wont go to school because of his stutter

Back on his bike Charlie will go
In the direction of Maitland Road
He's pedalling so fast because he can't be late
On his deliveries to the Merseybank estate

Merseybank, go in a tank
Because Charlie will flatten you
On his way to the bank
The bank in Merseybank
Is a fence called Frank
Known to locals as Nat West Frank

Charlie arrives at Frank's
With his bag full of swag
And they haggle over prices
In pounds, dollars and skag
They argue and curse each other into the night
A child of thirteen and a man of fifty five

Charlie leaves Franks
Pockets bulging with money

Laughing and giggling, thinking everything's funny
Stoned from the skunk Frank provided
In an effort to make Charlie lower his prices
Half-tripping he takes a ride around the marina
And he thinks of times when the grass was much
Greener
The still water much cleaner
His dad sober and his mum consolable
When big brother carried him everywhere on his
Back
Instead of the constant kicks and cracks
When school was just fun and bulging with joy
Chasing girls, climbing trees and stealing toys

Then, Charlie skins up, one for the road
And amidst the wildlife, foxes, people and toads
He dreams of a world
Less than a mile from all this madness
To the place where he carries out
The majority of his business
A peaceful place where it's warm and dark
But Charlie's thoughts go beyond the car park
He longs to lie there and be free from all the pain
Of his life growing up on the Merseybank estate

Charlie stands up, jumps on his bike
Pedals down the hill and along the jetty
Tears of joy in his eyes
His palms all sweaty
Then up in the air
A boy and his bike
He is putting an end to his miserable life
A loud splash
And Charlie lies at the bottom of the pond
Smiling happily, problems all gone

Beards

Southern Cemetery is the place
To take the smile off your face
Goodwins, take me down to Didsbury
With maximum haste
Because I've seen too much sadness
From Gorton all the way round
Goodwins, take me to a place
Where the people are more sound
Less uptight and twitchy
With eyes all intense
Goodwins take me to Didsbury
There's pounds, shillings and pence

Leafy green
Harris Tweed
Dogs with coats on
Cats on leads
Avenues and streets always clean
Rents and mortgages obscene
The kind of place where rich students' mums and dads
Buy their kids designer chilling pads
For their kids to chill in
For their kids to grin in
"Who are you fuckin' grinning at?"
Said the Burnage boy in the baseball cap
Snide Lauren hanging creased
Outside faded jeans
Adidas two-stripe really keen
"Leave it, Jason, he's a fuckin' queer"
Says Naomi slipping her tongue into Jason's ear
And running her neutralised fingers through his
Peroxide hair
But it is at the grinning man that Jason lustily stares
Then a volley of punches knocks the grinner to the
floor
And Jason runs off to lock his wardrobe door

The pubs effervesce
Fat men and women with beards
Tashes dripping CAMRA-recommended beers
Proudly boasting about their outdoor pursuits
Bright Berghaus at weekend
On weekdays a suit
"I ran the Pennine Way last week
Drove my 4 by 4 through mud four foot deep
My Decree Nisi arrived last Wednesday
Another pint of Old Peculiar mate?"

On Thursday it's grannies' fashion parade
Prozac and brandy chased by Lucozade
A trip out with a reason
Whatever the season
Wearing ornate hats and shoulder pads
Bright red lipstick
Towed by accessorised cats
Pouting and posing through the village catwalk
streets
Rubbing shoulders with bright Benetton beauties
Squeaky squeaky clean
Stoned, smiling and waving at passers by
Five hundred Queen Mothers vogue in one
Straight line
In the direction of the post office
Not to tax the civil list
But to cash in their vouchers and go on the piss
Ignored by their children for most of the year
They sit alone in their rotting real estate
Paralysed by loss and fear
So on Thursdays they dress up
Meet and have their say
Grey power in Didsbury on pension day

Stressed thirty-something's
In Volkswagen automobiles

Scream raucously at their kids
Tightly gripping the wheel
Late for work, got no fags
Totally wired
Twenty-hour days leave you constantly tired
The two tots are harnessed to their chairs
In the back
Nappies, bags and bottles crushing tiny laps
But the screams and the cries
That come from the rear
Is due to Mark Knopfler's guitar solo
Piercing young ears
And a prospect of a day
With a trainee nursery nurse
In an aesthetically pleasing nursery
Where managers curse
Toys sit on high shelves and children fall off chairs
The trainee nursery nurse pulls out her hair
Because parents don't listen
Too busy being snobby and moody
Aspiring to be like good old Richard and Judy
And buy a big house on Old Broadway
They'll have a heart attack at thirty-eight

There seems to be a lot of bigoted attitudes
And fat C2's who are horribly rude
To outsiders who like to drink here at night
Locals prod them, insult them
Force them to fight
Then complain to officer Dibble late into the night
There's a big fear that outsiders
Are trying to take over
The two words go well together
Didsbury
And Xenophobia

Reginald Varney

Finglands, Bullocks and GMT
Ten thousand buses coming at me
Headless people running round
Mostly youthful, heading for town
Rucksacks, holdalls, plastic bags
Hands scramble into pockets for their Marlboro
Light fags
A thumb flips a Zlippo
And its brown grinding wheel
Awakens me
This ain't a nightmare
This is real.

I'm on Wilmslow Road trying to catch a bus
Monday morning lecture time
The world is in a rush
Chaos reigns amongst broken glass

Because the leaders of tomorrow
Are late for class
Elbows dig into grannies ribs
Mamba, Samba, Bamba, Kick the mums with kids

"Do you go to the Uni
Do you go that way?"
The same questions asked everyday
And when it comes to pay the vendor
From the pocket comes a crisp, clean tenner
And no apology for the lack of change
Or for fucking up the driver's day

Scrambling through the throngs
Watch the brassneck dippers
Stand on the toes of the day-and-night trippers
Someone has stolen the disabled seat
Grannie's starting to buckle at the knees
While the ignorant sit in their comfy chair
Pondering life with out a care

"I really fancy Jordan
I really fancied Jack
I hope he's going to give me
My Oasis CD back
My head is throbbing
From the snakebites last night
All this drink makes me want to fight
Then I feel all depressed the following day
Struggling to make the pain go away
I'm lonely and don't know who my real friends are
I wish I could afford a nice little car
To run home and back, then here and there
I really liked Jack's with his reclining sporty chairs
But I haven't got the money to pay my rent
So I'll buy myself an enormous tent
And stick it in the middle of Platt Fields

By the boating lake and the bowling green
I'll start a commune that's what I'll do
And I'll ask Jordan if he wants to come too
Look at all these students
Making me late for class
No direction
No change
Pain in the ass"

More people jump on the bus
Escaping the rain
One guy looks soft and strange
Fixed and high
One shoe
One trainer
Tracksuit bottoms
Black donkey jacket
White shirt and black tie
His eyes are watery red and pained

And around his neck
A golden chain
With a large wooden crucifix
Different world
Different fix
His hair is matted, greasy and from his beard
Hangs sandwich crumbs
And mumbled tuneful words
His skin is brown but once was white
It comes from sleeping in parks at night
Growing up in twenty homes
Staring through windows at school
This man ponders life to a different set of rules
No Jordans or Jacks
Snakebites and black
Sports cars or reclining chairs
This man's mind is in despair
It is lost somewhere in the deep dark past
Between Captain Scarlet and sunday mass
He is in pain and grieving
Unable to tell what's wrong
So he keeps on singing and mumbling
His tuneful song

The bus takes off and it jerks and sways
Some kids have sneaked on forgetting to pay
"Who you fuckin' looking at you ugly dickhead?"
Said the ten-year-old boy with the shaven head
And the nauseous smell of Prioderm
That removes his nits but not the germs
Then the youngster intimidates a student
For a fag and a light
And jumps from the emergency exit
While the bus is in full flight

Bags seem to be everywhere
Rucksacks smack you in the face

Holdalls pile up on the stairs
There isn't space to put two feet on the ground
And you're not even halfway to town
And the smell of BO is bordering on obscene
Crammed into a 42 bus
Like freshly tinned sardines

Secretarial town girls
With orange faces thick with grease
Tut tunefully to town boys sat in the next seat
She prays for pay day because life's fast and hard
Trying to hide from her Access card
And keeping up with the Chantelle Jones's
Prada, Miss Sixty, Nike
Clothes for the lonely
Tatooed arse and pierced tongue
Knows some of the words to Chaka Khans songs
Knows all the dances and songs in the charts
Now she's off to file appointment cards

There's life on the bus
Driving through the Withington streets
Cine City's showing Trainspotting
Seven nights a week
A final effort before it's bought by contractors
To build luxury appartments to sell to rich actors
Who admire the streets with their northern grit
They're worse than poets for talking shit.

The bus is a place of anthropological study
Man in a travelling setting usually in a hurry
A rich tapestry of the working classes
With nothing to say
Just grinding Zippos
Ignoring each other
And plodding away.

The Fallow Field

In Fallowfield the dogs run the weed
There's a little compartment in the collar
Where they keep each deal
They run from house to house
And from street to street
To places that the tourists never choose to see
From Wilbraham Road down to Nursery Street
Where large avenues of people live in a vacuum
Listening to crackling transistor radios
Slapping out crackling chart tunes
From out of the window of a Cortina Mark II
With bricks for wheels
Because "The Milk" was overdue

The most beautiful girls that you have ever seen
Playing rallivoe, kerbie, kick-can and hide and seek
Kick can baby

HARDYS WELL
WAIT WATERLESS WANDERER WHOEVER WALKS
TO THE WELL WILL WADE INTO A WONDEROUS WORLD.
A WORLD WHICH WILL WAKEN THE WILTIN
WALLPAPER OF WORK AND WORRY. WELL WORRY
WILL WAIT WHILE WELLS WAND WHIRLS WARM-
HEARTED WACKINESS INTO A WEARY WEEK.
WHEREAFTER WAVES AND WATERFALLS (
WONDERMENT WILL WASH ALL WEAKNESS A WAY?
WELL? A WORLD WIDE WEB OF WHOLEHEARTED
WHOLESOME WISDOM AND WIT WAITS WHE AWAY
WORRIES. WELLS WORKS WOND   LES.
WHY WAIT. WHY WONDER. WHY
WAIN. WHY WHITTLE. WHY WITHE
WHAT WE WAITING FOR. IT'LL DO
HARDYS WELL.

One two three
Fighting with the lads and holding them tight
Dreaming of the evening and holding him right

Good jumble sales still happen round here
It's where Jack the lad
Gets all his going out gear
A bobbled Pringle jumper
That a golfer used to wear
Looks really sad in Albert Square
On one of the lads' big nights out
Doing geranies
Dipping jackets and blagging snouts
Minesweeping pints when their owners are
Up dancing
And at 1.45 the lads' start romancing
"It's quarter to two and I still haven't copped
It's probably because I'm totally off my box
And I can't really dance
I can only smooch
I just hold real tight and slowly move"

And there's loads of Mams
And there's Loads of prams
Trading Prozac for stories of painful mammary
Glands

And the same old words
Sometimes whispered
Sometimes blasted
"Why's my old man such a fuckin' bastard?"
Heroines every one of them
For the shit that they take
Rearing kids on a city council housing estate

Next door to the Library is a place known locally
As "Hell"
It's a 12 by 12-foot room
A Platt Lane police cell
Where bank clerks, Sunday footballers
And the innocent meet
After battles with Crumpsall on Oxford Street
But they're all laughing now
All joking with each other
Because one of the lads knows one of the other
Team's brothers
So they all meet in Fridays the following night
And take on Wythenshawe in the car park
In a massive fight

Outside Victoria Wine
Between the hours of eight and nine
A girl old enough to hustle
But no older than the time
Waits for a friendly face to come passing by
Then she'll ask them real coyly
"Can you do me a favour?
Get us ten B&H and a bottle of cider"
And she'll swear that they're for her
Bed-ridden mother
But she'll take them
Drink and smoke them down on Wilbraham Fields

She doesn't like the cigs
She doesn't like the cider
She likes the way it makes her feel
Lay on the grass
Staring up at the stars
A mind puddled and pickled
Helps massage the scars
A stagger through Aston and Clinton
And in the back door
Help her drunken father from the kitchen floor
Then falling up the stairs
On all fours to the small room
Head spinning and cheeks ballooned
Wrenching boak splatters Armitage Shanks
Heaving cider
The new chocolate and eventually blanks
Another child ploughed and harrowed
Left fallow for far too long
Too many hiding fathers
Too many crying mams.

Don't Rush Home

Jump on a bike and ride through fields to
Rusholme streets
Watch nippers playing on street corners
With magic carpets, such a treat
Cycle down Coronation Streets time after time
Dodge the dogs
Dodge the dickheads
But do not be blind
To the beauty that surrounds
Special people
Special smells
Special sounds
More than an aura

There's a bitch outside a butchers
Hoping for a bone
Dreaming of an elephants graveyard
And her ascendancy to the throne
Meanwhile, Little Johnny waits
Outside Gregg's bakery
He's sucking the cuffs of his jumble sale jumper
Because it's pasties again for tea
And Mona smokes and asks imaginary blokes
For a ticket to her show inside their mind
And an alley that vomits X reg Datsuns
And big fat white behinds
Julie's screaming at simple Stephen
About the money he's been stealing
About the shit he's been dealing
She says she's gonna leave him
Then she screams "I'm fuckin' leaving"
Its cold and it's grey
Like A Play for Today

I drop two gears on my mountain bike
And nearly fall off

And the sound of Betjeman is booming
From two old codgers on a croft
Pictures of Tony Blair hang on locals'
And students' walls
Dog shit every colour of the rainbow
Trees in Platt Fields fall
While City and the council are working in cahoots
Like United, it's not footy
It's just businessmen in suits
Brown envelopes here, strange transfers there
And shoot the suit in the Director's chair
But the most heinous of crimes was committed in
Trafford Park
Where money-making bastards banished real
Fans to The dark

Boscombe Street
Heald Place
Eileen Avenue
Victory Street
Claremont Road
Wilmslow Road too
Whitworth Park
MRI and art galleries
Peel back your eyelids
Open the mind
Learn to see
Marx and Engels used to drink round here
Pondering poverty
Commenting that the locals had reached
And I quote, "The lowest stage of humanity"
Riots that you've never fucking heard of
Massacres that sound like wars
Peterloo and starving rioters
White slavery on Plymouth Grove

This is the last and greatest democratic city
Where radicalism was born out of people being shit on

Trade Unions, the Labour Party the Chartist
Movement
Were organised in back bedrooms
Now rented to students
Defining radicalism without ever meaning to
Making walking down the street easier for me
And you
The Pankhursts plotted for women's rights
Down on Nelson Street
And on Plymouth Grove there's a house
Where Gaskell and Bronte used to meet
Orwell was down and out in Longsight
While De Quincey climbed the walls
Marvin Gaye only came for the day
Because he couldn't score at all

Cycle further past the BBC
Getting closer to the city

City Living

In sunless piazza
In silver furnished windswept shady collonades
In bars where nothing ever happens
And beer is only sold by the half
Freshly grated chocolate floats
Then slowly melts into a white artificial effervesence
That will be sipped, slurped and dabbed
From the lips of the beautiful people
The movers and shakers
The makers and breakers
The fifteen-minute mateys
The no givers only takers

Ad men in pastel brainstorm for their latest campaign
Selling Manchester without the rain
An umbrella the size of the county
Will be deployed
And cloud busters will be positioned in Chadderton,
Heaton Moor, Urmston and Hyde
All rain dancers will be rounded up, baubled to stop
Them boogieing out of town
Then, brick by brick, sod by sod and mound by mound
The Pennines will be taken down

Project team two are from the Evening News
On the case of misinformation
Or selling a tale
As they did with deck access
Olympic bids
Anderton and the Arndale
Colour supplement sells King Street paved with gold
Where everything's pristine and scrubbed
And no-one is old
No-one is fat and everyone is pretty
And you'll be like a celebrity if you shop in this city

Project team three are from the BBC
KEY 103 and Granada TV
And their role is to report on Manchester
With a stupid fucking grin
Shots and soundbites on location
Sell to the nation
A city paved in sunshine and smiles
And Fred says, there's not a single raindrop to be
Found for twenty miles

Pretty pictures of Catalonian Castlefield
Sell seven sisters sipping spanish sangria
And latino and jazz are the sounds that we hear
Beamed like shit from the arse of a dog
With diarrhoea

The final project team is known as property
Fat boys at the bar drinking Stella
Second generation something or other
Bought a terraced in Rusholme
50 - 50 with his brother
Rented it to students
Then he bought another gaff
And all he's done since then is laugh
Bought a plot of land, backhanded for planning
Permission
Now him and his brother are on a property mission
Bought old mills for peanuts - just his department
Grants from the council to build luxury appartments
Now they've bought the garage, a playground
And a section of the park
And all they've done since then is laugh
Now they're getting ready to buy the grey sky
Cos there's nothing left here to buy

And God Created Wythenshawe

Adam and Eve walk down Princess Parkway
Their lives possessions on the back of a pony and
cart. Slum clearance has taken them to
Wythenshawe. They are building a new life.

Eve Dreams - 1960

Show me a way out
A world without grey
Without gloom
Dark damp and cold
Show me a summer breeze
That makes small children smile excitedly
I have lived in the darkness too long

Show me a toilet inside a house
Something green not black
Show me space and movement
Give me the right to hold my arms open wide
To embrace the things I love
I have lived in the cold too long

Show me steam from hot water
As it trickles into a white bath
Show me the tears in your eyes when you laugh
Show me ponds, lakes, rivers that run to the sea
Give me a chance to find the real me
I have lived amongst gloom too long

Show me gardens and trees
Lawns that stretch as far as the eye can see
Take a photograph of you with me - smiling
Fresh air that saves the children with coughs
Show me a television, show me a shop

My diet of gruel has gone on for too long
Show me schools and books
Streets without trucks
Roses and daffodils smiling and swaying
Nippers on streets with footballs playing
I have lived with the sadness too long

Show me birds and butterflies
Not tears of sadness in the children's eyes
Broken promises and landlords' lies
Show me a place where I can think
With fresh water to drink
Clean air to breathe
Help me to believe that this can be real
Show me a way out

Jacobs Rant - 1980

Show me the things that we were promised
By the powers-that-be
Show me the garden city
Show me roses blooming proud in pink
Moist petals quivering in the winds of change
Show me bees buzzing

Show me humming birds
Humming the tune to Land of Hope and Glory
Show me chrysants
In the fists of fat maiden aunts
Red faced from morning milking
Show me fuchsia fighting for a front-row seat
In The theatre of promises
The secret garden of dreams that someone
Locked the gates to, then threw away the key
Show me butterflies on willow branches
Waif-like wings opening and closing in their
Twilight days
Show me waters from streams
Reservoirs and rivers
Show me it as it runs into the Mersey
And out to the Irish sea
Show me thin stones skimmed across a lake
In the thumbs and forefingers of teenagers
With reason
Not two fingers pointing skywards
Show me canoodling teenagers in long grass
In the shadow of an oak
Honest promises not broken dreams

Don't show me men in grey suits
Playing trivial pursuits
With the people of Wythenshawe
Don't show me whippersnappers
Just out of nappies
Now in ties
And half-button flies of trousers too big for them
Don't show me brown envelopes
Penned poisoned notes
From town halls a million miles from here
Making decisions about people they don't know
But somehow fear

Show me an autumn leaf
Crisp not green
Golden brown and wrapping its arms around Itself
Watch it fall to earth
Floating slowly
In peace
Watch it rise again on a breeze
Twisting and turning
Spiralling
Surveying the world without eyes
Absorbing thought and words
Through oceans of time.

Show me a Y-shaped prop
Holding a washing line high into the sky
Show me white sheets doubled over and folded
Billowing white cotton bleached by summer sun
Starch dry

Images of summertime
Fields and dreams
Children's laughs and screams
Kids running through long grass
Cold to the touch
Just running in silence
Cold to the touch
Angry and frightened
Cold to the touch

Show me what we were told we'd see
Don't show me fields replaced by concrete
Parks covered by tarmac
The sound of swallows drowned out by shadows
And a petroleum filled bird screeching overhead
As its nest grow and grows
Show me the things we were promised by the
powers that be
Where is the Garden City?

Show me Hope - 2000

Show me hope
Ambition
The desire to achieve
A lust for life
Show me opportunities being seized upon
With both hands clasping tight
Taking our chances
Having a go
Nowt to lose
Everything to gain

Show me dignity and pride
A sense of belonging not existing
Go with the wings of change
Take a chance, don't resist it
Show me people working together for change
Not fighting over parking space in the
Pissing rain
Or kicking the dog because the bus is late again

Show me rebuilding without buildings
And the regeneration of generations of
generations of generations of underachievement
Show me people living honestly and free
Show me fathers taking responsibility
Not duckin' and divin'
Dodging and weaving
Dodgy dealing
Show me dads sat with their kids reading
Not red in the face from bawling and screaming
Cos a dog or a horse or a goal didn't come in

Show me the library heaving
Show me dads talking to children
Telling them things you wish your dad told you
Give them something to do - with you
Give them something to believe in
Beyond the motorway din
Show me Mams taking responsibility
Asking questions of fathers on mobile phones
"Are you staying out or are you coming home?
Why do you always want to be on your own?
Why do I feel so alone?
Do you know the names of all your children?
Can you give me an idea of how I'm supposed to
Feed them?
What has happened to all that ambition?"

Show me people telling the kids that they can
That there's nothing they can't do
That they can achieve anything they want
With a bit of hard work
And a bit of support

Show me men and women leading by example
Don't get caught up in life's violent scramble
Or living in the bookies
Taking the gamble

Down at bingo but never shouting house
And panic sets in as your felt pens run out
Queueing for lottery tickets you'll put in the bin
Always lose never win
And those scratchcard dreams of hope and glory
Same old numbers
Same old story
Don't drown these sorrows with Stella and spliff
And watch your dreams slowly soused
And smoked
Watch your dreams soaked and smoked
Watch your dreams showered and baked
Drenched and burned, tossed and turned

Show me a new world
Working for change
And in the words of JFK
Ask not what this city can do for you
Ask what you can do for this city

Show me hope
Don't show me pity

Embarrassed to be Half English

I'm embarrassed to be half-English
I feel totally ashamed
When reading through these history books
The facts I read are plain
English men once stalked this earth
With cannons, swords and guns
And stuck a Union Jack in any ground they set upon
The cunning of the bully meant
Rule Britannia ruled the waves
And let us not forget England's key role in the slave
Trade
The slavery continues
But now the slaves wear suits
Suffer with negative equity
And on Thursday scan through loot
For a decent double buggy
The twins are due in June
The slavery continues
Look at me, then look at you

I'm embarrassed to he half-English
When I look at the Queen
Pink and blue and fluffy
Looking totally obscene
I think of what she symbolises
An unelected head of state
And it's just another reason for this boiling vat
Of hate that bubbles up from within
When I think of this place called England
That we're expected to live in

I'm embarrassed to be half-English
With its Care in the Community
Ignoring the most in need in total unity
And the way the sick and the old

Are made to beg for pension and dole
Whilst living in fear of being mugged or attacked
To pump up the heroin or smoke some crack

I'm embarrassed to be half-English
Watching the English abroad
Red skin
Lager
HP beans
Union Jack shorts
Cultureless, tasteless bastards
Singing football songs in tune
And fighting for The national flag
While fifteen cockney's moon
And a shag's a shag on holiday
Is the kind of thing the English say

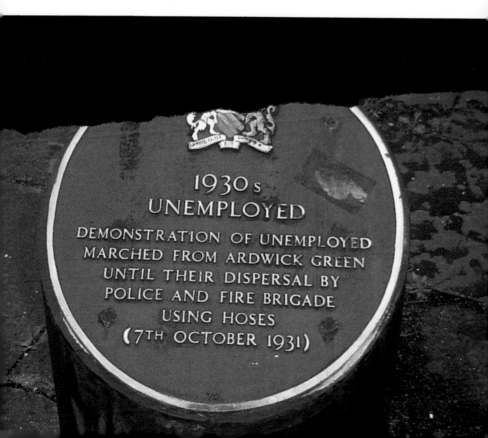

I'm embarrassed to be half-English
Walking through the city streets
Muggers, rapists, bandits, burglars and thieves
Stand in line in a queue
To mug rape burgal and thieve
From the likes of me and you
And the kids are swigging cider
Cos there's nothing else to do
And the kids are smoking Ganja
Cos there's nothing else to do
And the kids are getting excluded
Cos there's nothing else to do

I'm embarrassed to be half-english
Aren't you?

Think about it

I don't want to
Think about
These things that I've been
Thinking about
Cos when I
Think about
The things I
Think about
I think, don't think about it
Think about something else
Think about something that won't make you
Think about
The things you dont want to think about
Think about it

Books published by Cheers Ta

Men's Morning Holden Caulfield
Isbn 0 9536392 0 7
£4.99

Amongst the madness of the
innercity is a sanctuary. A sauna,
where a group of men meet every
friday to work rest and play.
Men's morning is poetic tale of
how men escape the drudgery of
life through sport, sweat and
conversation.

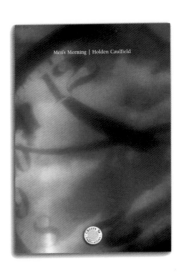

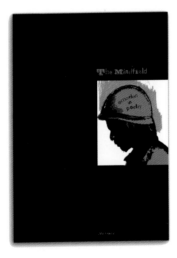

The Mindfield Dike Omeje
Isbn 0 9536392 1 5
£7.99

The first collection from a truly
original wordsmith. A master of
performance and slam poetry.
The Mindfield captures the best of
his live show in book form.
"This man's rhymes will not be
denied, a serious thinker at work."
- Pete Kalu

To order any of these book
call 07970 158 191 or order online at www.cheersta.co.uk